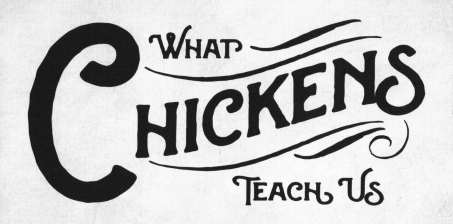

What Chickens Teach Us

WHAT CHICKENS

TEACH US

WITH ADVICE FROM THE HENHOUSE

▨ WILLOW CREEK PRESS®

Published by Willow Creek Press, Inc.
P.O. Box 147, Minocqua, Wisconsin 54548

All Photos © shutterstock.com except page 2 © McPhoto/agefotostock.com and page 4 © Topic Photo Agency In/agefotostock.com

Printed in China

Enjoy simply being outside in the

fresh air &

Sunshine

Arise early and celebrate the first sunshine, the first breeze, the first smell of flowers.

But mornings would be a lot more fun if they didn't come so Early

Take your responsibilities seriously.

When you're the center of attention,
it's hard to be
Humble

Each morning marks a new beginning and a full day of new opportunities.

You can't soar with the eagles without first flapping your wings.

There's no place like Home

Have confidence in yourself and, put a little spring in your step.

Be Thankful when someone extends a hand

We should all try to spend
more time at the beach.

Include lots of leafy greens in your diet.

There's never been anyone on earth quite like you.

Free range is fine,
just don't take it too far.

Look both ways before crossing the road, to see what's on the other side.

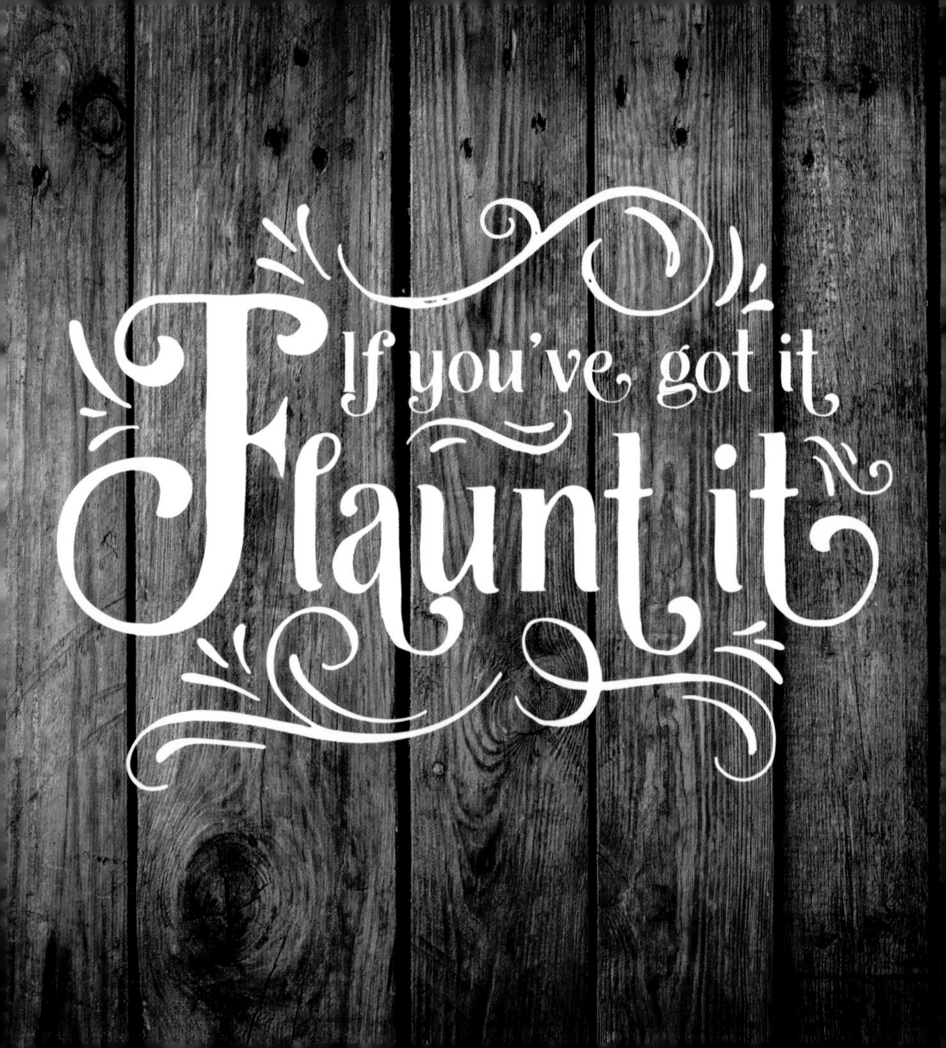
If you've got it
Flaunt it

If you keep watching the world go by, it will.

Start each morning with a simple, leisurely breakfast.

Just because we're not all alike doesn't mean we can't all like each other.

Break away from the Crowd, and try something Extraordinary

Seize the hay!

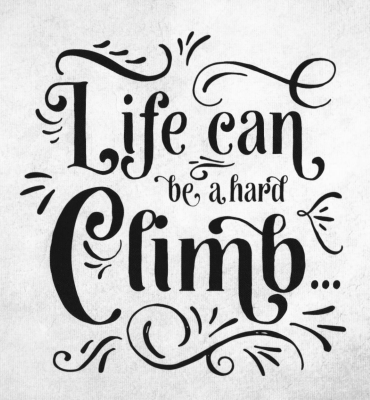

Life can be a hard Climb...

...but it's a pretty nice view
from the top of the heap.

Try
to keep adding to the
Nest Egg

Opportunities are like sunrises—
wait, too long, you miss them.

It's always a good idea to follow the straight & narrow

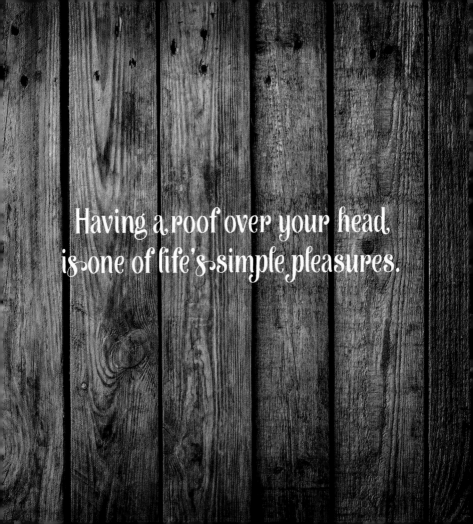

Having a roof over your head,
is one of life's simple pleasures.

Conformity is a fashion crime.
Dress for yourself and for comfort.

Life is Short

recognize each new day as the gift that it is

The grass really IS greener
on the other side of the fence.

Even if you don't have a song

Sing

For every door that closes

Another
one
Opens

Try viewing things from
a new perspective.

Count your chickens after they **Hatch** and you'll never be disappointed

Don't be timid—speak up when you have something to say.

The best way to lead is by Example